Seasons

A Book of Poetry About Sweets, Treats, and Random Feats

by Nikita Lalwani

ISBN
978-1-4602-3000-8 (Paperback)
978-1-4602-3001-5 (eBook)

Produced by:

FriesenPress
Suite 300 – 852 Fort Street
Victoria, BC, Canada V8W 1H8

www.friesenpress.com

Distributed to the trade by The Ingram Book Company

Table of Contents

Spring

April showers,
Bring flowers.
Easter day,
Month of May.
Strawberries,
Ripe cherries.
Chinese New Year,
Season of deer.
Week of break,
Bears that wake.
Birds that sing,
Bees that sting.
Cherry blossoms,
Furry possums.
Leaflet buds,
Growing spuds.
Outdoor sports,
Colored shorts.
Cold ice teas,
Greener trees.
Spring has sprung,
Fun's just begun.

Nikita Lalwani

Summer

Swimming pool,
Feeling cool.
Ferris wheel,
Orange peel.
Ice-cream pops,
Soft flip flops.
Whirring fans,
Golden tans.
Volleyball,
And the mall.
Sandy dunes,
Soothing tunes.
Crowded beach,
Juicy peach.
Lemonade,
In the shade.
Basil time,
Lemon lime.
Water slide,
Soothing tide.
Sleeping in,
Dark burnt skin.
Summer fun,
For everyone.

Nikita Lalwani

Autumn

Colored trees,
Scattered leaves.
Big pumpkin,
Chilly skin.
Windy nights,
Small frostbites.
Shorter days,
Cornfield maze.
Apple juice,
Stuffed up goose.
Thanksgiving,
Brown stuffing.
Halloween,
Ghosts are seen.
Carving tools,
Pumpkins rule.
Back to school,
Jeans are cool.
Straw scarecrow,
Crops to grow.
Warmly dressed,
Peaceful rest.

Nikita Lalwani

Winter

Frosty bites,
Shiny lights.
Cup of Joe,
Ho, ho, ho!
Christmas Day,
On a sleigh.
Chilly night,
Snow that's white.
Jolly smiles,
Presents pile.
Marshmallow,
Hot cocoa.
Cute kittens,
Soft mittens.
Slushy boots,
Owl hoots.
Warm clothes,
Frozen toes.
Carols to sing,
Next up, Spring!

Nikita Lalwani

Eric McBrown

There's a new kid in town,
His name is Eric McBrown.
He goes to our school,
And is anything but cool.
When he walks, he gawks,
When he stomps, he chomps.
He has big chubby hands,
And slouches when he stands.
He falls asleep in class,
And hogs my hall pass.
His friends call him greedy,
His teacher says he's needy.
Sometimes he's mean,
And he never looks clean.
He's a bully in the hall,
Because people trip and fall,
When Eric McBrown walks by.
There's a new kid in town,
His name is Eric McBrown,
We hope he leaves as quickly as he got here.

Nikita Lalwani

A Winter Treat

When you're outside in winter, looking for a treat,
Drink some hot chocolate, it's really sweet!
The liquid is warm, like a hot tub in summer,
But if it gets cold, that's a real bummer.
The ooey gooey marshmallows are so great,
That your eager tongue just can't wait.
Don't forget the frothy whipped cream,
Soft and fluffy, just like a dream.
You're out in the snow, with a frozen nose,
Shivering as the icy wind blows.
You slip your hand out of your coat,
And pour the liquid down your throat.
Gulp! Slurp! You feel all tingly inside,
That freezing cold feeling starts to hide.
When you're outside in winter, looking for a treat,
Drink some hot chocolate, it's really sweet!

The Monkey in the Tree

There's a monkey in that tree!
He climbs as high as the eye can see.
Tiptoeing across the canopies,
He's only as tall as your knees.
He shrieks with laughter racing through the tree tops,
If he's not careful, he will surely drop.
He eats berries with his smelly feet,
But bananas are his monkey treat.
When the monkey climbs down from the tree,
He scampers straight towards me.
He climbs my shoulder and looks me in the eye,
There's a smile on his face, and I let out a sigh.
He hugs me tight, and shrieks goodbye.
There's a monkey in that tree,
And my friend he'll always be.

Nikita Lalwani

A Trip to Grandma's

The yellow taxi drops me off,
The engine stops, with a cough.
I pay the man and lift my bags,
And stop and stare at the house's flags.
I ring the bell, and step aside,
And sneeze at the odor of pesticide.
The doorknob turns, and she comes out,
Holding a steaming, yummy trout.
She pulls me close, and says in my ear,
"Hello Sam, I'm glad you're here".
I push past her, and run inside,
I quickly find a place to hide.
Grandma shrieks, "Want some pie?"
I shudder, shake, and start to cry.
She walks towards my hiding spot,
I curl up in a helpless knot.
She stretches out her hand for me to see,
I think she's closing in on me.
Suddenly, I see some pie,
I take it, with a huge sigh.
I come out from under the table,
I almost trip on a telephone cable.
She hugs me and says, "Sam, don't worry,"
I walk to the kitchen, and sniff some curry.
She kisses me, gentle as a fairy,
Then I knew grandma wasn't scary.

Nikita Lalwani

School

Endless stairs,
Lots of chairs.
Diet Coke,
Funny joke.
Fraction test,
Smartly dressed.
Gross spit balls,
Parent calls.
Inking pens,
Loyal friends.
Pointy tools,
Pesky rules.
Teacher's pet,
Stage is set.
Kitchen food,
Lovely mood.
Smelly feet,
Meet and greet.
Buzzing phones,
Loud trombones.
Bubblegum,
Noisy drum.
Troubling grades,
Awesome parades.

Nikita Lalwani

Ghosts

Ghosts are creepy,
They make me weepy.
Their pitch-black hollow eyes,
Remind me of devious spies.
Their creepy white skin,
Makes my head spin.
All their howls and screams,
Give me horrible dreams.
They skulk around the hall,
But never trip and fall.
They hover in the air,
And sneak up for a scare.
They're shapeless and their legs are gone,
Their cackling fills the house at dawn.
If you come close, they'll snack on you,
Then disappear without a clue!
They like to prank you just for fun,
If you see one, you should run.
Ghosts are spooky, but have no fear,
They're just fake, not really here.

Nikita Lalwani

Planet Baloo

There are strange things on Planet Baloo,
Like the 82-petaled flower called the Hitzeroo.
An 18-legged monster named Finny,
And a double-nosed ant named Linny.
With really weird grass that eats your toe,
And when it's full, it starts to glow!
There are Martians that enjoy playing cards,
Accompanied by their bodyguards.
There are no vegetables on Planet Baloo,
So the residents eat stew made with bamboo.
Instead of using doors, Baloonies break through walls,
And citizens play with cubes instead of balls!
There are unusual drinks that make you fly,
And really gross foods that give you a black eye.
All the creatures have a flashlight,
So no one gets a terrible fright.
Their language is very simple and the only word is "ooo",
But if you say it with a chirp people understand you.
Their ruler is a worm and his name is Min,
When people pass by, they flash him a grin.
There are very strange things on Planet Baloo,
I hope when you visit, you can understand "Too".

Nikita Lalwani

Sports

Basketball,
Deadly fall.
Diving blocks,
Muddy socks.
Colored shoes,
Painful bruise.
Scoring goals,
Balls in holes.
Drenched in sweat,
Soccer net.
Coach's frown,
Sweet touchdown.
Knotted cleats,
Track meets.
Hole-in-one,
Scalding sun.
Massive splash,
Speedy dash.
Twirling spines,
Finish lines.
Balance beam,
The 'A' team.

Nikita Lalwani

A Sweet Trip to Heaven

There are many delightful tastes in sugary treats,
Like those scrumptious lollipops.
And those marvelous chilled ice-cream cones,
Like mouth-watering milk chocolates.
And warm soothing hot chocolate with whipped cream,
Like the sour tangy sensation of sour patch.
And the sickly sweet taste of chewy marshmallows,
Like the colorful taste of candy canes.
And the cleansing, fresh feeling of white mints,
Like the soft melted chocolate chips in home-made cookies.
And the cold icy feeling of grape popsicles on a summer day,
Like the popping spine-tingling taste in jellybeans.
And moist fluffy chocolate cake with frosting,
Like the fizzy bursting banging energy of Nerds.
And the wild crazy feeling of Airheads,
Like the super creamy caramel taste in maple doughnuts.
And the sweet crumbly warmth of Oreo's,
So if you like the myriad tastes of sugar.
You have a sweet tooth.
So go ahead and send your taste buds on a trip to heaven,
Where all your sugary dreams come true.

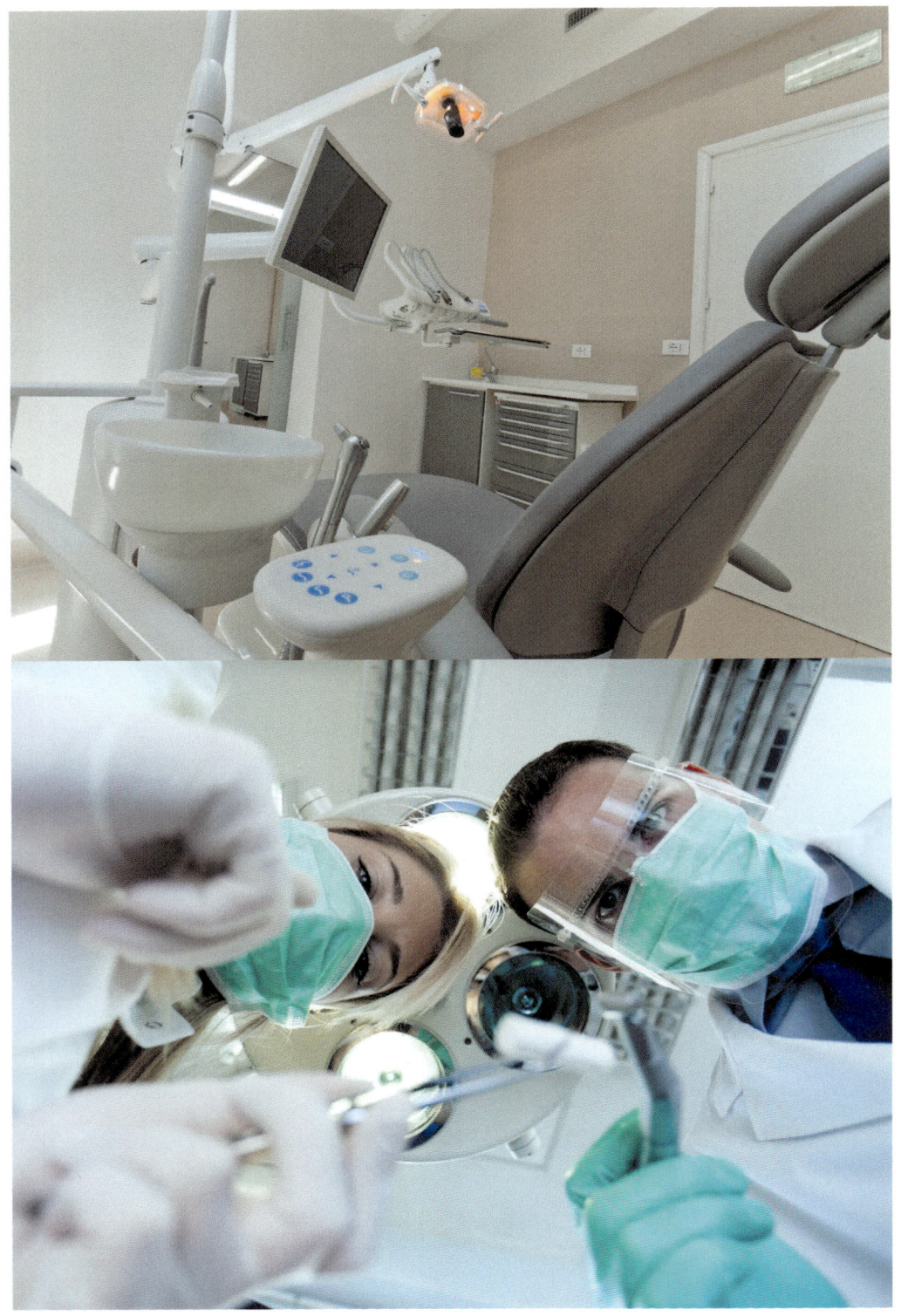

Nikita Lalwani

The Dentist's Office

My mom yanks me out of the car,
I latch onto the seatbelt bar.
She pulls me off and takes me away,
My vision starts to swirl and sway.
She takes me through the big glass door,
I cannot take it anymore.
The elevator starts to soar,
I scream and let out one big roar.
We stop on the seventh storey,
I think this is about to get gory.
I walk inside and see the man,
Above him whirrs a giant fan.
He says hello and takes me inside,
I start to get all teary-eyed.
I take a seat on the chair,
He's giving me a huge scare.
He approaches me with his metal stick,
His gloves purple and very thick.
He scrapes and scrubs my teeth with grace,
I know there's tears flowing down my face.
The nurse shoves in gooey fluoride,
The saliva in my mouth has dried.
He leaves my chair and I scream with joy,
The nurse hands me a little toy.
My mom gives me a big high-five,
I'm really glad that I'm alive.

Nikita Lalwani

The Race of a Lifetime

I'm about to have a running race,
There are beads of sweat pouring down my face.
I line up at the starting line,
I think I will do just fine.
We take our marks and the gunshot sounds,
The blood in my head starts to pound.
Number four has taken the lead,
I really need to bump up speed.
Then number seven sprints in front,
I hear her start to groan and grunt.
I pick up speed and sprint ahead,
If I go faster I might be dead.
Number seven trips on her shoe,
She falls down with her face all blue.
I then catch up to number four,
She starts to sprint even more.
Then number three slows down,
Her face has on a big huge frown.
I pass her with a cunning grin,
I think that I am going to win.
Number eight comes deadly close,
I say to her, "adios".
I jump across the finish line,
That golden trophy is all mine!
I dance across the grassy land,
The trophy shining in my hand.

Nikita Lalwani

The Mall

Oh my gosh, I'm at the mall,
I want to buy stuff, I want it all!
I want that glitzy pink lipstick,
And the nail polish that looks very slick.
Or a chocolate ice-cream cone,
And that stylish new cell phone.
Plus those earrings up for sale,
Or that adorable blue whale.
Don't forget that fragrant rose,
And a pedicure for my toes!
Or those multi-colored bands,
And some rings for my hands.
I also want that unicorn,
Or that book called 'Firethorn'.
Look at that cool girlish hat,
I really want to buy that!
Or that pretty golden pet fish,
And that shiny porcelain dish.
Look at those dazzling slippers,
And those yellow flippers.
At the mall, there's so much stuff,
Like bedtime pillows with tons of fluff.
When I see the mall, I say "Wow",
But sadly, Christmas is a year from now.

Nikita Lalwani

Sweet Treats

Cream on top,
Nerds that pop.
Minty gum,
Cookie crumb.
Powdered dips,
Sugared lips.
Frosted flakes,
Homemade cakes.
Sugar cubes,
Chocolate tubes.
Gooey treats,
Yummy sweets.
Candy batch,
Sour patch.
Candy cane,
Gummy brain.
Jellybean,
Halloween.
Ice-cream cone,
Dreamy scone.
I'm hasty,
'Cause sugar is tasty.

Nikita Lalwani

The Sea

I took a trip under the sea,
All the creatures really stunned me.
I saw a silky baby shark,
With eyes so bright, they had a spark,
I glanced upon some orange coral,
That looked to me very floral.
I passed a speedy flying fish,
His tail was carving a big swish.
I spied an eel with eyes so clear,
I was thankful for my diving gear.
There was a turtle far away,
And a Great White hunting for prey.
A clown fish swam under my feet,
I think it was looking for food to eat.
An octopus latched onto my arm,
I hope he won't cause any harm!
But then he finally let go,
And latched himself onto my toe.
I broke loose and swam far from there,
That octopus gave me one big scare!
I was swept onto the coral reef,
And I gently sighed with sweet relief.
Paddling up to the top,
I surfaced with a plop.
I took a trip under the sea,
Where there were many things to see.

Nikita Lalwani

The Nightmare Station

I met my friend for a celebration,
After I got the invitation.
I used my transportation,
To get to the strange location.
The house had decoration,
Like a holiday sensation.
We used our imagination,
To play with participation.
After careful communication,
Appeared a scientist who taught animation,
And gave us an education.
The wall was colored like a carnation,
A truly amazing creation!
We watched a movie called *"Zombification"*
That gave us hallucinations.
To calm down we did some meditation,
Which really helped our relaxation.
There was chocolate cake for temptation,
That vanished and left starvation.
Then the pipes burst and there was dehydration,
The party was turning into a nightmare station,
So I left without hesitation,
And headed home in desperation.
I woke up, covered in perspiration.

Nikita Lalwani

Christmas Day

Snow is out on the ground,
Kids are frolicking all around.
I lift the hot chocolate to my lips,
While my dog constantly yips.
Snowflakes kiss my frozen cheeks,
These are the biggest in weeks.
Christmas lights flicker on and off,
And the icy wind makes me cough.
I hear the jingle of silver bells,
And turn to see Santa with a smile that's swell.
Ho, ho, ho, and he's on my chimney top,
Rudolph slows down, and comes to a stop.
Santa disappears, and delivers a gift,
In a minute or so, he's back to his shift.
I walk inside my house with a grin,
And dust the snow from my frosted chin.
My dog takes a nap beside the warm, glowing fire,
And the smoke from my chimney rises higher and higher.
I wake up to the sound of a sleigh,
And to my delight, it's Christmas day.

About the Author

Nikita Lalwani lives in Portland, Oregon, U.S.A. where she attends middle school. This is her first collection of poetry, and she is working on her next book in between homework assignments. She loves writing, swimming, playing the piano, and spending time with her family.

Lightning Source UK Ltd.
Milton Keynes UK
UKIC01n0045200315
248205UK00002B/7